Contents

What is a sunflower?. 4

Spring. 6

1–2 weeks. 8

4–6 weeks. 10

6–8 weeks. 12

9 weeks. 14

Summer 16

10 weeks. 18

13 weeks. 20

14 weeks. 22

16 weeks. 24

A field of sunflowers 26

Life cycle 28

Fact file 30

Glossary 31

Index 32

What is a sunflower?

There are many kinds of sunflowers.

Sunflowers are tall plants with large, flat flowers. They can be many different colours. Sunflowers come from North America but now grow in other parts of the world too.

3 days

1 week

6 weeks

These plants are the most common kind of sunflower.

The most common kind of sunflower has bright yellow petals. In this book, we will find out about the life cycle of this kind of sunflower. All sunflowers grow from large seeds.

8 weeks

10 weeks

13 weeks

Spring

A sunflower seed has a striped pattern on it.

The sunflower seed is planted in the ground in spring. The soil is warm and damp so the seed will grow well. Inside each seed is a new plant which soon begins to grow.

3 days

1 week

6 weeks

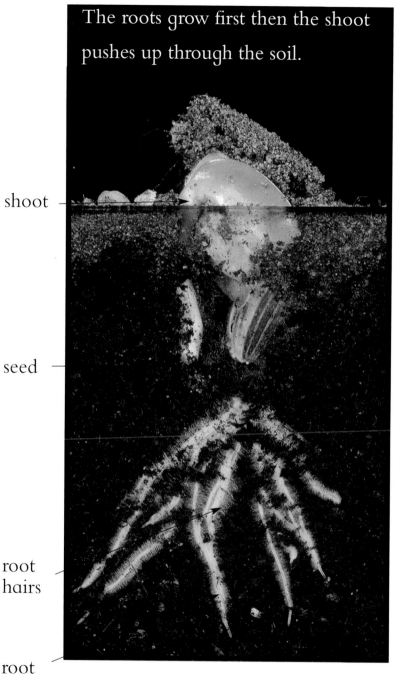

The roots grow first then the shoot pushes up through the soil.

shoot

seed

root hairs

root

The **roots** start to push down through the soil. Look at the roots of this plant. They are covered in tiny hairs. These tiny root hairs take in water.

A green **shoot** appears next. The shoot grows upwards.

7

8 weeks

10 weeks

13 weeks

1–2 weeks

Between one and two weeks, the green **shoot** has pushed through the soil. The new leaves open out. Now that the leaves have opened out, they can start to make food for the plant.

Leaves use sunlight, air and water to make food for a plant.

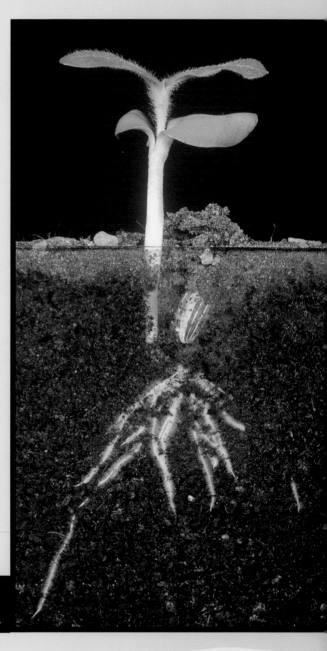

The new leaves start to make food for the plant.

The plant grows much taller now.

The new sunflower plant grows taller. More leaves grow at the tip of the **stem**. Look at the stem in this picture. It has fine hairs on it to stop insects from climbing up it.

fine hairs

stem

9

8 weeks   10 weeks   13 weeks

4–6 weeks

The sunflower leaves grow bigger and the roots grow longer.

Now the sunflower leaves are much bigger. Under the ground, the **roots** grow longer. The roots take in water and **minerals**. The plant needs water and minerals to stay alive and keep growing.

3 days   1 week   6 weeks

The bracts protect the new bud.

bract

Soon a large **bud** grows at the end of the **stem**. The bud is protected by pointed green **bracts**. Bracts look like small leaves.

8 weeks

10 weeks

13 weeks

6–8 weeks

As the **bud** grows the **bracts** unfold. The bud starts to open.

bract

The bracts unfold and the bud begins to open.

3 days   1 week   6 weeks

By eight weeks, the sunflower bud is beginning to open. Now the bright yellow petals can be seen.

There are bright yellow petals underneath the bracts.

13

8 weeks

10 weeks

13 weeks

9 weeks

flower-head

The plant grows taller and taller. The flowers open out. Each **flower-head** contains many tiny flowers.

In 1986 a very, very tall sunflower was grown in Holland. The sunflower grew to 7.76 metres! That's almost as tall as two double-decker buses!

Each flower-head is made up of many tiny flowers.

3 days

1 week

6 weeks

Sunflowers turn their flower-heads to face the Sun.

All the sunflowers turn to face the Sun. As the Sun moves across the sky, the flower-heads turn to follow it.

8 weeks

10 weeks

13 weeks

Summer

pollen

Each flower-head is made up of tiny florets.

florets

Each **flower-head** is made up of hundreds of tiny flowers. These tiny flowers are called **florets**. The tips of the florets are covered with a fine yellow dust called **pollen**.

3 days

1 week

6 weeks

Honey bees collect pollen from the flower-head.

The flower-head is growing bigger. Honey bees see the bright yellow petals and come to the flower-head to collect pollen.

A sunflower that grew in Canada in 1983, had a huge flower-head. It was 82 cms across. That's bigger than a car wheel.

17

8 weeks

10 weeks

13 weeks

10 weeks

This bee gets covered in pollen as it crawls across the flower-head.

As the honey bee crawls across the **florets**, its body and legs become covered in **pollen**. The bee flies from one **flower-head** to another. It collects a lot of pollen.

3 days

1 week

6 weeks

The pollen rubs off the bee's body into the florets.

As the bee crawls from one floret to the next, pollen rubs off its body into another floret.

In the middle of each floret, there is a tiny **ovule**. The ovule becomes a seed when the **pollen** joins with it. This is called pollination.

19

8 weeks

10 weeks

13 weeks

13 weeks

The petals around the flower-head start to wilt.

By 13 weeks, the **florets** have no pollen left. But, inside each floret, a seed starts to swell. The petals around the **flower-head** are no longer needed. They wilt, die and fall off the flower-head.

3 days

1 week

6 weeks

These flower-heads are so heavy with seeds that they are drooping.

21

The flower-heads become darker and turn almost black. The flower-heads are very heavy with all the seeds growing inside them. Some become so heavy that they droop from the end of the **stems**.

8 weeks

10 weeks

13 weeks

14 weeks

Now the flower-head is a mass of shiny, black seeds.

By 14 weeks, the **florets** start to wither, too. The **flower-head** is now a flat disk of hundreds of shiny, black seeds.

Birds like to feed on sunflower seeds.

Birds feed on the seeds. The seeds pass through the birds' bodies. Some of the seeds may land on good soil. When it is warmer again, in the spring, these seeds may grow into new plants.

8 weeks

10 weeks

13 weeks

16 weeks

The harvester cuts the plants and shakes out the seeds.

At 16 weeks, it is time to **harvest** the sunflower seeds. The farmer drives a machine called a harvester. The harvester cuts the plants and shakes out the seeds.

3 days

1 week

6 weeks

The harvester missed this plant!

Some plants are missed by the harvester. This plant was missed. Now the leaves wither and die. The seeds drop onto the ground. Some of the seeds may grow into new plants next spring.

8 weeks

10 weeks

13 weeks

A field of sunflowers

This farmer's field has a good crop of sunflowers.

Sunflowers are grown for their seeds. Farmers plant huge fields of sunflowers so they can get a big **crop** of seeds. Many seeds are crushed and then made into animal feed. Most seeds are squeezed to make sunflower oil.

Many people like to eat sunflower seeds. Roasted sunflower seeds make a good snack. Pet guinea pigs like to eat sunflower seeds, too. But a farmer never sells all the seeds he has grown. Some seeds are kept to be planted next spring.

Life cycle

3 days

1 week

6 weeks

8 weeks

10 weeks

13 weeks

Fact file

Sunflowers can grow over 7 metres tall. That's taller than a one-storey house!

The **flower-head** can be 30 to 40 centimetres across. That's as big as a dinner plate.

Each flower-head may produce 1000 seeds. Most seeds are made into oil and margarine.

Sunflowers grow all over the world but more are grown in Russia than in any other country.

Glossary

bracts   parts of a plant that protect the bud while it grows. In most other kinds of flowers they are called sepals

bud   a flower before it opens

crop   plants that are grown to sell

floret   a tiny flower, which is part of a flower-head

flower-head   a flower that is made up of many tiny florets

harvest   to gather in ripe crops

minerals   chemicals that the plant needs to stay healthy

ovule   female egg that forms a seed when joined with a male pollen

pollen   the tiny male seeds of a plant

roots   the parts of a plant that grow under the ground and take in water

shoot   a new or young growth on a plant

stem   the part of a plant from which the leaves and flowers grow

Index

bracts   11, 12, 13
bud   11, 12
florets   16, 18–20, 22
flower-head   14–18, 20–22, 30
flowers   14, 15, 16
leaves   8, 9, 10, 11, 25
ovule   19
petals   5, 13, 17, 20
pollen   16–19
roots   7, 10
seeds   5, 6, 20–27, 30
shoot   7, 8
soil   6, 7, 8
stem   9, 11, 21